Piano Music of
BÉLA BARTÓK

The Archive Edition
Edited by Dr. Benjamin Suchoff

SERIES II

Piano Music of
BÉLA BARTÓK

The Archive Edition
Edited by Dr. Benjamin Suchoff

SERIES II

Dover Publications, Inc.
New York

The present volume is part of the publication program of the New York Bartók Archive, to include both Studies in Musicology and the Archive Edition of Bartók's music itself. The complete series of works is projected as follows:

STUDIES IN MUSICOLOGY

BENJAMIN SUCHOFF, Editor

The Béla Bartók Archives: History and Catalogue

Rumanian Folk Music
I Instrumental Melodies
II Vocal Melodies
III Texts
IV Carols and Christmas Songs (*Colinde*)
V Maramureş County

Turkish Folk Music from Asia Minor

Béla Bartók Essays

Yugoslav Folk Music
I Serbo-Croatian Folk Songs (*with Albert B. Lord*)
II Tabulation of Material
III Source Melodies: Part One
IV Source Melodies: Part Two

The Hungarian Folk Song

THE ARCHIVE EDITION

I Piano Music of Béla Bartók, Series I (Dover, 1981)
II Piano Music of Béla Bartók, Series II (Dover, 1981)
III Songs
IV Orchestral Works
V Chamber Works
VI Music for Chorus
VII Instrumental Pieces

Piano Music of Béla Bartók, Series II is a new work, first published by Dover Publications, Inc., in 1981.

International Standard Book Number: 0-486-24109-2
Library of Congress Catalog Card Number: 80-70402

Manufactured in the United States of America
Dover Publications, Inc.
31 East 2nd Street, Mineola, N.Y. 11501

CONTENTS

THREE BURLESQUES, OP. 8C / *81*

FOUR DIRGES, OP. 9A / *100*

TWO PICTURES, OP. 10 / *108*

THE FIRST TERM AT THE PIANO / *134*

SONATINA / *144*

INTRODUCTION

The Archive Edition of Bartók's works is an extension of the New York Bartók Archive Studies in Musicology publication series. The Archive Edition is intended to serve the public—for the first time!—with the authentic performing version of Béla Bartók's early compositions, published during his lifetime or posthumously in Hungary, and those other, heretofore unpublished works which were found among his other memorabilia subsequent to his death in New York City on September 26, 1945.

Two principles have guided the preparation of the Archive Edition, both of them expressed by Bartók himself:

"It is of great importance that anyone who is involved with music should be able to obtain [composers'] works in editions which interpret precisely the author's intentions, not of such kind that may have been arbitrarily modified or forged by some adapter" [*Béla Bartók Essays*, No. 82, p. 499].

"To place [this material] before the public as carefully prepared and in as perfect a form as is called for by its unparalleled value" [*Rumanian Folk Music*, Vol. I, p. 2].

When Bartók emigrated to the United States in October 1940, he brought with him the bulk of his compositions and folk-music collections, in manuscript and published form. The Archive Edition is based on his own corrected publications or, whenever such materials were missing from his memorabilia, on original editions in the New York Bartók Archive. In the latter case, comparative study was made between them and new editions published in Hungary since 1951; these recent publications apparently have made use of holdings in the Budapest Bartók Archivum.

The present publication was produced by direct photographing of the above-mentioned original editions. Editorial addenda are enclosed in square brackets in the musical part, and square brackets are also used for Bartók's duration indications at the end of certain pieces.

Although the Archive Edition is performance-oriented, the editorial annotations that follow below reflect musicological scholarship based on primary source materials, in the expectation that this publication can serve as an intermediary stage in the future preparations of the Complete and Critical Edition of Bartók works. These annotations are intended to provide an aid to interpretation of Bartók's music and further the understanding and appreciation of the man as composer.

FOR CHILDREN

COMPOSITION DATE: 1908–1909.

FIRST PERFORMANCE: Perhaps Kecskemét, Hungary, 1 February 1913.

FIRST PUBLICATION: Rozsnyai Károly, Budapest, 1909–1911.

In 1907, four years after his graduation from the Academy of Music in Budapest, Bartók was offered the chair of piano teaching there to succeed his own teacher, István Thomán. Bartók was happy to accept the position since it would enable him to settle in Hungary and continue his studies in musical folklore. The next year Karóly Rozsnyai, the Budapest music publisher, contracted with him to edit Bach works for piano and compose easy pieces for the instrument. In the latter category the first contract—for *Ten Easy Pieces* (included in the companion volume to this one, *Piano Music of Béla Bartók*, Series I)—is dated 25 June. The next contract, dated 23 March 1909, is for 21 "juvenile music pieces" to be titled *For Children*.

This first volume, based on Hungarian musical folklore and apparently delivered to Rozsnyai on or about the contract date, was quickly followed by a second volume of similarly oriented pieces (contract dated 23 June). On 10 November 1910 Bartók signed an agreement for the publication of Vol. III of *For Children*, this time based on Slovak musical folklore; and on 9 May 1911 an agreement for Vol. IV, the last in the series, also devoted to Slovak material.

It is interesting to note the publisher's comments in a letter, dated 6 December 1909, that was enclosed with the newly printed works: "I wish to emphasize that it would be better if the rules of classical harmony were even more strictly observed without any modernization than in the ones already published. I should not like to see a new trend in this undertaking but rather the beaten track on which you can continue working from time to time . . . ." As one scholar has observed, Bartók's rejection of Rozsnyai's conservative taste is proved by the compositions of the last two (Slovak) volumes of *For Children*, which deviate even more radically from the rules of so-called classical harmony than those of the first two volumes.

It should be emphasized, however, that the composer's creative processes were not guided by pique but by the demands of the materials with which he was working: "East European folk music, generally, avoids allusions to the dominant triad in its melodic structure [the familiar reciprocity of effect between tonal and dominant is voided by melodic lines based on the old ecclesiastic and pentatonic modes], thereby allowing in its harmonization a much more extended liberty."

Shortly after Bartók emigrated to the United States in October 1940, he prepared a program that combined a piano recital with a lecture titled "Contemporary Music and Piano Teaching (the role and importance of contemporary music in the piano teaching of today, with explanatory examples on the piano)." This lecture, presented at various American colleges and universities, included 16 pieces from *For Children* (Bartók's lecture notes indicate only that he performed Nos. III, X, XIII, XIX, XXI, XXXII, XXXIII, XXXIV and perhaps XL from the first two [Hungarian] volumes):*

> Already at the very beginning of my career as a composer I had the idea of writing some easy works for piano students. This idea originated in my experience as a piano teacher; I had always the feeling that the available material, especially for beginners, has no real musical value, with the exception of very few works—for instance, Bach's easiest pieces and Schumann's *Jugendalbum*. I thought these works to be insufficient, and so, more than thirty years ago, I myself tried to write some easy piano pieces. At that time the best thing to do would be to use folk tunes. Folk melodies, in general, have great musical value; so, at least the thematical value would be secured. The following sixteen pieces are some of these piano pieces based on folk tunes.
>
> I will begin with a group of eight pieces; all these are very easy, pupils can easily play them in the first or second year of their studies. The folk tunes used in them are of simpler structure, some of them having even an almost international character. So they do not present to the beginners any special difficulty and can be easily grasped by them. [Bartók performance.]
>
> The following eight pieces are taken from the same collection but are somewhat more difficult; they may be played in the third or fourth year. [Bartók performance.]
>
> These sixteen pieces are taken from my work entitled "For Children," which contains about eighty pieces. I wrote them in order to acquaint the piano-studying children with the simple and non-romantic beauties of folk music. Excepting this purpose, there is no special plan in this work.

Bartók's reference to "about eighty pieces" seems to indicate that he was then anticipating a revision of *For Children*, since the first version contains 85 compositions. Three years later, in November 1943, his publisher, Boosey & Hawkes, wrote to him as follows:

> *Pieces for Children*: I discussed the matter with our lawyer and he has no doubt but that we can obtain a copyright for the pieces if you make some slight alterations. He is quite satisfied that the alterations as discussed at our meeting the other day will be sufficient and I would therefore ask you to kindly go ahead and prepare the pieces for an early publication. As soon as you are ready let me know and I will come to get the manuscript from you.

Bartók speedily completed his alterations, and on 21 December 1943 the publisher reported: "We started work on the CHILDRENS PIECES and I hope to be able to send you proofs within a few weeks." The new version of *For Children*, published posthumously in 1946, contains 40 pieces in the first (Hungarian) volume and 39 in the second (Slovak) one. Omitted pieces: Nos. XXV and XXIX (Hungarian material), 23, 27, 33 and 34 (Slovak material). It should be noted that Nos. 33 and 34 were composed by Emma Sándor, Zoltán Kodály's first wife.

For Children, in its entirety, is representative of the first level in Bartók's approach to the transmutation of folk music

into art music: "The used folk melody is the more important part of the work. The added accompaniment and eventual preludes and postludes may be considered as the mounting of a jewel." He also believed it to be more difficult to write a transcription than to compose an original work: "In some cases the use of a given theme presents greater difficulty because of the restriction given by it. In any case, in order to write a good transcription, the composer must have creative imagination at his disposal as well, quite as much as in the writing of an original work. When the restrictions of using the simplest means are put on the composer, the difficulty increases. For, generally, restrictions demand greater mastery of technique."

Those pieces in the present publication designated by the Roman numerals I to XXXXII are based on Hungarian folk songs, collected for the most part by Bartók himself in 1906 and 1907. His study of this and other material eventuated in a substantial number of books and articles in which he was the first to point to Hungarian musical folklore as falling into three major categories for classification purposes:

(A) Old-style melodies of ancient origin, for the most part characterized by *parlando-rubato* (free, declamatory) rhythm; four-line text stanzas of equal syllabic length, in ABCD sectional form; pentatonic scale (transposed to g^1 as final tone):

in which a^1 and e^2 appear as passing tones or graces; and the final tone of the second (main) section mostly on the (lowered) third degree of the scale, less often on the fifth or first degrees.

(B) New-style melodies that came into being probably in the early 1850s, and whose prevalent features include *tempo giusto* (strict) dance rhythm; architectonic or rounded form, mostly ABBA content-structure; ecclesiastic modes and the modern major scale; the final tone of the second section almost always on the fifth degree of the scale; and extensive use of so-called "dotted" (that is, syncopated) rhythm patterns:

(C) Mixed-style melodies, which either lack certain characteristics peculiar to those in Class A or Class B, or possess stylistic features borrowed from foreign sources—Czech, Moravian, Ruthenian (Ukrainian) and Slovak materials. As a case in point, the Ukrainian *kolomyjka* dance-melodies, with their characteristic 4 + 4 + 4 + 2 syllabic structure:

probably were the source for Hungarian herdsmen's songs and dances (see Nos. XXXIX and XXXXII, below).

Included in the original edition of *For Children*, Vols. I and II, are appendices containing the related Hungarian folk-song texts and collection data. The texts, English translations and other editorial commentaries are provided below in the numerical order of the published melodies. Immediately following this listing is the discussion and similar editorial treatment of the Slovak material in Vols. III and IV.*

---

*Bartók's own published copy of *For Children* shows two sets of numbers: 2. 4. 3. 10. 6. 7. 11. 4. and 13. 19. 20. 21. 32. 33.

*A detailed comparison of the original and revised editions of *For Children* will be found in the recording of the work, Hungaroton LPX 11394-95.

PART ONE
(Vols. I and II)
MELODIES FROM HUNGARIAN CHILDREN'S AND FOLK SONGS

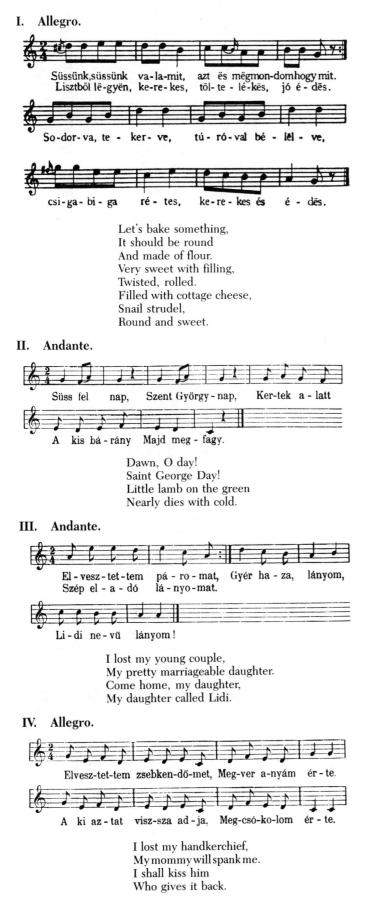

I. Allegro.

Süssünk, süssünk va-la-mit,   azt ës mëgmon-domhogy mit.
Lisztből lë-gyën, ke-re-kes,   töl-te-lë-kës, jó é-dës.

So-dor-va, te-ker-ve,   tú-ró-val bé-lël-ve,

csi-ga-bi-ga   ré-tes,   ke-re-kes és   é-dës.

> Let's bake something,
> It should be round
> And made of flour.
> Very sweet with filling,
> Twisted, rolled.
> Filled with cottage cheese,
> Snail strudel,
> Round and sweet.

II. Andante.

Süss fel   nap,   Szent György-nap,   Ker-tek a-latt

A kis bá-rány   Majd meg-fagy.

> Dawn, O day!
> Saint George Day!
> Little lamb on the green
> Nearly dies with cold.

III. Andante.

El-vesz-tet-tem   pá-ro-mat,   Gyér ha-za,   lányom,
Szép el-a-dó   lá-nyo-mat.

Li-di ne-vű   lányom!

> I lost my young couple,
> My pretty marriageable daughter.
> Come home, my daughter,
> My daughter called Lidi.

IV. Allegro.

Elvesz-tet-tem zsebken-dő-met,   Meg-ver a-nyám ér-te.

A ki az-tat   visz-sza ad-ja,   Meg-csó-ko-lom ér-te.

> I lost my handkerchief,
> My mommy will spank me.
> I shall kiss him
> Who gives it back.

V. Poco Allegretto.

Cziczkom, Cziczkom, Va-gyon-e szép lá-nyod? Add ne-kem
Va-gyon, va-gyon, De mi hasz-na va-gyon.

azt, El-ka-pom azt. Szi-ta szi-ta pén-tek, Sze-re-lem csü-
(Rivalom)

tör-tök, Dob szer-da.   A le-gények re-gi-ment-je I-gen

czif-ra, Ben-ne fo-rog Sán-dor Pan-ka,   I-gen nyal-ka!

I-cze u-cza Re-be-ka, De é-kes a de-re-ka,
Ha é-kes is,   il-le-ti,   Bar-na le-gény sze-re-ti;

Ga-lam-bocs-ka.   Mint a csont-ka.
Ga-lam-bocs-ka,

> Kitty, kitty, have you a pretty girl?
> I have, I have, but what is it good for?
> Give her to me, I take her,
> Sieve, sieve Friday, love Thursday, drum Wednesday.
>
> The lads' regiment is very showy,
> The dashing Sándor Panka—in it!
> Itsa, utsa Rebecca, how bedecked her waist,
> Lovey-dovey.
> Though bedecked, she wiggles it;
> A dark lad loves her,
> Lovey-dovey.

VI. Allegro.

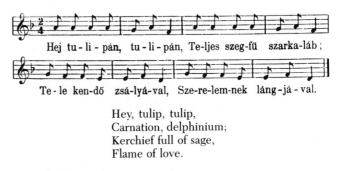

Hej tu-li-pán, tu-li-pán, Te-ljes szeg-fű szarka-láb;

Te-le ken-dő zsá-lyá-val, Sze-re-lem-nek láng-já-val.

> Hey, tulip, tulip,
> Carnation, delphinium;
> Kerchief full of sage,
> Flame of love.

VII. Andante grazioso.

1. Ke-resd meg a   tűt,   én meg a gyü-szűt,

had vargyam meg a ba-bámnak a per-gál ün-git.

> Look for the needle,
> And I for the thimble,
> That I may sew
> The percale shirt of my sweetheart.
>
> I have sewn it already,
> Put it on him already;
> His two suntanned cheeks
> I have kissed already.

This piece is an example of the "heterogeneous kind of melody [mixed style: Class C] which more or less points to a presumable infiltration of Western European musical culture."

VIII. Allegretto.

Hey, *görbénye, görbénye,*
What are you doing in the village?
Give, give
To poor *görbénye*
That he might go, might go
In the town's cellar!

I am a priest, I am a craftsman,
You are permitted to say one or two words,
That one who will laugh
Must put up something as a pledge.

IX. Molto Adagio.

White lily,
Hey! jump into the Tisza [river]!
Hey! jump into the Danube!

Lean on your side,
Against the big pitchfork!
Hey! trim yourself nicely!
Hey! wash yourself nicely!
Rub yourself nicely!

X. Allegro molto.

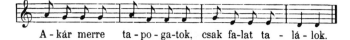

The Walachians, the Walachians wear wooden shoes;
A good time is had by those who walk by twos.
See! I, poor journeyman, walk by myself;
Wherever I reach, I touch but a wall.

XI. Molto sostenuto.

I lost my young couple,
My pretty marriageable daughter.
Give me my young couple,
My pretty marriageable daughter.

A mixed-style melody (see the comment to No. VII, above).

XII. Allegro.

Chain, chain, floral chain,
My floral chain, thread,
Thread, even if silk,
It would be discarded.

Ring, ring would be money
Or my friend, Mariska, Mariska
Turn in the fashion of angels.

XIII. Andante.

The following folk song, from Bartók's study *The Hungarian Folk Song* (see References), is a variant of the source melody used for the piano transcription (both tune and text were known throughout Hungary):

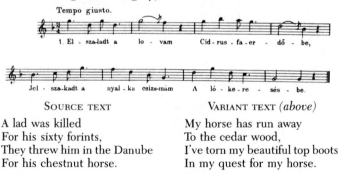

SOURCE TEXT	VARIANT TEXT *(above)*
A lad was killed	My horse has run away
For his sixty forints,	To the cedar wood,
They threw him in the Danube	I've torn my beautiful top boots
For his chestnut horse.	In my quest for my horse.

Bartók placed this piece among the mixed-style (Class C) melodies, although it has the Old Hungarian characteristics of pentatonic mode, ending of the second (main) melody section on b^1 flat, and the so-called "dotted" (syncopated) rhythm. However, the four heterometric lines (6, 6, 8, 6 syllables), even though of ABCD content-structure, disallows its placement among old-style Hungarian folk songs.

XIV. Allegretto.

The poor lads of Csanád
Stole a goose.
They caught it by the neck, by the neck, by the neck,
So that it began to gaggle.

A Hungarian folk tune in the new style (Class B), known throughout the country.

XV. Allegro.

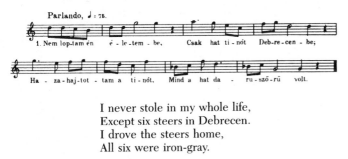

SOURCE TEXT

Teeny-weeny is the street of Istvánd,
Something is still there that lures my heart;
Coming and going, I pass there, too;
My little one is still far away.

VARIANT TEXT (*above*)

This little girl's frock is too short;
I said to her mother, "Sew flounces round it."
She said to me, "I'll sew no flounces round it;
Who disapproves need not walk after her!"

A Hungarian folk tune in the new style (Class B), known throughout the country.

XVI. Andante rubato.

I never stole in my whole life,
Except six steers in Debrecen.
I drove the steers home,
All six were iron-gray.

An Old Hungarian (Class A) folk tune.

XVII. Adagio.

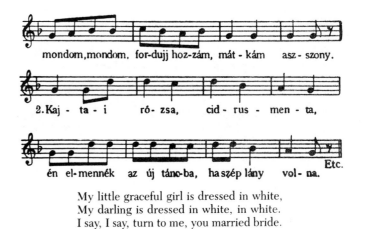

My little graceful girl is dressed in white,
My darling is dressed in white, in white.
I say, I say, turn to me, you married bride.

XVIII. Andante non molto.

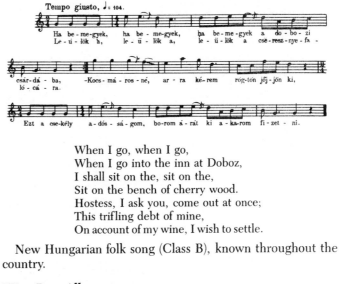

SOURCE TEXT

A warship lies in the harbor of Nagyvárad,
The national flag flies amidships and on her four ends.
The wind blows it, blows it homeward,
The infantrymen of '01 [1901] await their discharge.

VARIANT TEXT (*above*)

At the landing at Nagyvárad stops the steamship,
Over her floats the country's flag.
Blowing wind, unfurl it towards our country,
For we old soldiers all together are going on furlough.

A very widespread New Hungarian (Class B) folk song.

XIX. Allegretto.

When I go, when I go,
When I go into the inn at Doboz,
I shall sit on the, sit on the,
Sit on the bench of cherry wood.
Hostess, I ask you, come out at once;
This trifling debt of mine,
On account of my wine, I wish to settle.

New Hungarian folk song (Class B), known throughout the country.

XX. Poco Allegro.

The street of Ürög is straight;
Friend, you'll find no pretty maid there,
All who live there are hunchbacked,
The corners of their mouths are jagged.

The source text is unsuitable for publication. Old Hungarian folk song (Class A) which shows transposing-structure: the second half of the melody (bars 7–12) is approximately a repetition of the first half, lower by a fifth.

XXI. Allegro robusto.

Poco parlando ♩ = 80

Ëggyik ágy-ba pet-re-zse-lëm, a má-sik-ba zel-ler,

Kocsmá-ros-né szó-gá-ló-ját mëg-tosz-ta ja kel-ler.

I-há-ni, ci-gá-ri, jó be-lő-le pi-pá-nyi,

Ha-ja dá-ri, ma-dá-ri, jó be-lő-le pi-pá-nyi.

Text translation unsuitable for publication.

XXII. Allegretto.

One ought to go to Debrecen,
One ought to buy a turkey cock.
Watch out, carman, the cage has a hole,
The turkey cock will fall out.

A variant of the tune, transcribed for piano, appears in Elemér Limbay's collection *1200 Magyar Dal (-Album)*, published by Henry Litolff's Verlag, Braunschweig (the first edition was published in six volumes, between 1879 and 1888, in Hungary):

Allegretto.

Bartók's transcription is of the source melody, a children's song known throughout Hungary. The melody, of the mixed-style (Class C) type, probably originated in Germany, where it was sung there in parallel thirds (as in bars 1–2, 4–6 in the music example above). When such tunes were taken over by peoples who practice unison singing only, one of the parts (usually the lower) was left out.

XXIII. Allegro grazioso.

1. Igy këll jár-ni, úgy këll jár-ni,
2. Fogd a kon-tyot, hogy ne lóg-jon,

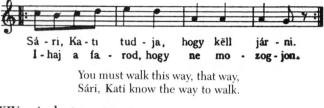

Sá-ri, Ka-ti tud-ja, hogy këll jár-ni.
I-haj a fa-rod, hogy ne mo-zog-jon.

You must walk this way, that way,
Sári, Kati know the way to walk.

XXIV. Andante sostenuto.

Víz, víz, víz, nincsen o-jan víz, mint a Kö-rös-víz,

Har-csa, csu-ka la-kik benne, Szép mënyecske fürdik ben-ne,

Víz, víz, víz, nincsen o-jan víz, mint a Kö-rös-víz.

Water, water, water,
There is no other water,
Like the Körös' water.
Catfish, pike live in it,
Pretty young wife swims in it.

XXV. Allegro.

Three apples plus a half,
I asked you, you didn't come;
If you didn't come, you stayed there.
Became the mother of girls.

The following variant, transcribed for piano, appears in Limbay's collection (publication details in the commentary to No. XXII, above):

Allegretto.

XXVI. Andante.

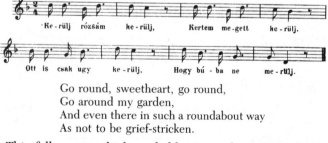

Ke-rülj rózsám ke-rülj, Kertem me-gett ke-rülj.

Ott is csak ugy ke-rülj, Hogy bú-ba ne me-rülj.

Go round, sweetheart, go round,
Go around my garden,
And even there in such a roundabout way
As not to be grief-stricken.

This folk song, which probably stems from Transylvania, appears in István Bartalus' collection *Magyar Népdalok* (Budapest: Rózsavölgyi és Társa), Vol. III, p. 127; see also Vol. IV,

p. 76), which was published in seven volumes—for the most part with piano accompaniments—between 1873 and 1896.

XXVII. Allegramente.

The source text and melody are unavailable. The following variant, transcribed for piano, appears in Limbay's collection (publication details in the commentary to No. XXII, above):

A mixed-style melody (see the comment to No. VII, above).

XXVIII. Parlando.

The source text (melody unavailable) appears in the following variant:

> László Fehér stole a horse
> Beyond the black hill.
> László Fehér was caught there
> And put into the depth of jail.

A mixed-style melody (see the comment to No. VII, above).

XXIX. Allegro.

> Oh! Hey! What do you say?
> Supper for the girls,
> Stuffed goose leg.

From Ádám Horváth Pálóczi's song collection of 1813 (edited by Dénes Bartha and József Kiss, and published by Akadémiai Kiadó, Budapest, 1953).

XXX. Andante.

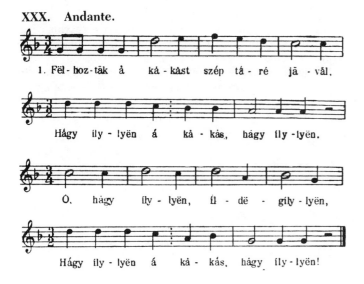

> They brought up the rooster with his beautiful comb;
> That the rooster be alive, be alive.

> Oh, that he be alive, live on;
> That the rooster be alive, be alive.

> We give the head to the bigwigs;
> That the rooster be alive, be alive.

> We give the neck to the stiff-necked;
> That the rooster be alive, be alive.

XXXI. Allegro scherzando (source melody unavailable).

> Mother, dear mother,
> My boots are torn,
> My boots are torn,
> Who will sew them right now?

XXXII. Allegro ironico.

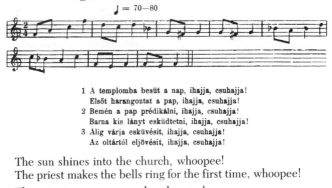

> 1 A templomba besüt a nap, ihajja, csuhajja!
>   Elsőt harangoztat a pap, ihajja, csuhajja!
> 2 Bemén a pap prédikálni, ihajja, csuhajja!
>   Barna kis lányt esküdtetni, ihajja, csuhajja!
> 3 Alig várja esküvésit, ihajja, csuhajja!
>   Az oltártól eljővésit, ihajja, csuhajja!

> The sun shines into the church, whoopee!
> The priest makes the bells ring for the first time, whoopee!

> The priest enters to preach, whoopee!
> To marry the little brunette girl, whoopee!

> She hardly can wait to be wed, whoopee!
> To leave the altar, whoopee!

A mixed-style melody (see the comment to No. VII, above).

XXXIII. Andante sostenuto.

> Stars, stars, brightly shine,
> Show the way to the poor fellows;
> To the poor fellows show the way,
> Or they won't reach the house of their love.

New Hungarian (Class B) folk song.

XXXIV. Andante.

> My ox is eating the aftergrass,
> When he has done I'll tie him up;
> Then I'll go to my sweetheart,
> I know that she awaits me.

SOURCE TEXT

> White lady's eardrop [*Fuchsia coccinea*],
> Don't come in broad daylight;
> Come in the evening,
> Icu [Nell?], dear, that I may look into your eyes.

VARIANT TEXT (*above*)

> My ox is eating the aftergrass,
> When he has done I'll tie him up;
> Then I'll go to my sweetheart,
> I know that she awaits me.

An Old Hungarian (Class A) folk tune.

XXXV. Allegro non troppo.

Ker-be vi-rá - got szëd-tem, lá-bam ösz-sze-tör-tem,

De jól ad-ta az Is-ten, hogy fér-hëz nem mën-tem.

Fér-hëz mën - tem vol-na, rossz u-ram lëtt vol-na,

Más-tól fél - tëtt vol-na, sok-szor mëgvert vol-na.

I picked flowers in the garden, I bruised my feet,
God granted me not to be married.
If I would have married, I would have had a bad husband,
He would have been jealous, would have flogged me often.

XXXVI. Allegretto.

Jaj de szé-pen e - sik az e - ső, Jaj de szé-pen zöl -dül a me - ző,

Kö-ze-pi-be le-gel a ju-hom,— Ka-to-na jaz é - des ga-lam-bom.

SOURCE TEXT

Margitta is not far away,
I drive there in an iron car;
Iron car, the linchpin is of copper,
My sweetheart's name is secret.

VARIANT TEXT (*above*)

Alas, how beautifully falls the rain!
Alas, how beautifully green is the field!
Around me my flock is grazing,—
My beloved, alas, is soldiering.

New Hungarian (Class B) folk song.

XXXVII. Poco vivace.

Ki -do-bo-zi ke-rek er-dő de ma-gos, Kö - ze-pi-be bar - na kis lány

a - ra-nyos. Hogy-ha én az er - dő-nek a szél-ső fá-ja

le - het - nék, A ba-bám-nak vál-la-i - ra bo - rul - nék.

SOURCE TEXT

When I go up Buda's big mountain,
I see under me Kis-Szele's center;
I see there, I see there the girls of Kis-Szele,
Their shoulders covered with pearl festoons.

VARIANT TEXT (*above*)

Around Kisdoboz is a high forest,
In it is a gold-brown maiden.
If I could be the farthest tree in this forest,
I would rest upon my love's shoulder!

New Hungarian (Class B) folk song.

XXXVIII. [Vivace.]

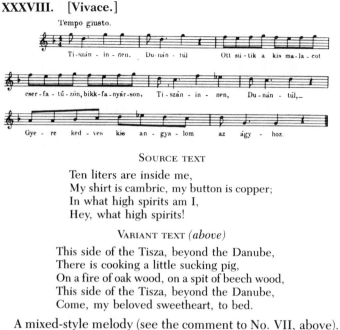

Ti-szán - in - nen. Du-nán - túl Ott sü-tik a kis ma-la-cot

cser-fa - tü - zön, bikk-fa-nyár-son, Ti-szán - in - nen, Du-nán - túl,—

Gye - re ked - ves kis an - gya-lom az ágy - hoz.

SOURCE TEXT

Ten liters are inside me,
My shirt is cambric, my button is copper;
In what high spirits am I,
Hey, what high spirits!

VARIANT TEXT (*above*)

This side of the Tisza, beyond the Danube,
There is cooking a little sucking pig,
On a fire of oak wood, on a spit of beech wood,
This side of the Tisza, beyond the Danube,
Come, my beloved sweetheart, to bed.

A mixed-style melody (see the comment to No. VII, above).

XXXIX. Allegro.

-Csó - ri ka-nász mit főz-tél? —Tü-dőt ká-posz - tá - val.

-Mi-vel rán-tot - tál be-le? -Ha - sa - sza-lon - ná - val.

-Hát az ö - reg e - szik-e? Tőtsd ne-ki tál - ba.

Ha nem e - szik be - lő - le, vágd a po - fá - já - ho!

SOURCE TEXT

The cricket marries, he weds the gnat's daughter.
The louse hurry-scurries, wants to give the bride away.
The flea dashes forward, wants to be best man;
All kinds of smelly bugs want to be guests.

VARIANT TEXT (*above*)

"Swineherd of Csór, what are you cooking?" "Lights with cabbage."
"And how are you cooking them?" "With fat."
"Then the old man will eat it? Fill the dish for him.
If he does not eat out of the dish, hit him on the cheek."

A mixed-style (Class C) melody in *kolomyjka* rhythm. The *Kolomyjka* is a Ruthenian or Ukrainian dance tune whose rhythm schema is twelve eighth-notes followed by two quarter-notes, in duple meter. Hungarian variants show different syllabic structure in certain cases (7 + 6, 7 + 5, 8 + 5 syllables), and their texts indicate the possible use of the *kolomyjka* as tunes for the Hungarian *kanász* (swineherds') dances.

XL. Molto vivace.

Agy-gyon az úr-is-ten en-nek a há-zi-gaz-dá-nak

Két kis ök - röt *stb.*

Haj re-gő rej-të, j azt is mëg-en-ged-të a nagy úr-is-ten.

May the Lord give
To the head of this household
Two little oxen.
Hey, *regö rejtë,**
Our great Lord has granted that, too!

XXXXI. Allegro moderato.

"Do you go, darling?" "I should think so!"
"Do you leave me?" "Certainly!"
"If you go, so shall I,
We both should leave!"

An Old Hungarian (Class A) folk song.

XXXXII. Allegro vivace.

This variant of No. XXXIX (above), also collected by Bartók in the village of Felsőiregh (Tolna County), was performed on the *furulya* (the well-known peasant or shepherd's flute; a pipe made of one piece of wood) by an old man who was the last of his kind in the village. As previously mentioned, this tune is a mixed-style (Class C) melody in *kolomyjka* rhythm, used in Hungarian swineherds' (*kanász*) dances. This piece is unaltered peasant-flute music, transcribed from the on-the-spot recording (Record No. 55 in the Budapest Ethnographic Museum) and provided with piano accompaniment.

PART TWO
(Vols. III and IV)
MELODIES FROM SLOVAK CHILDREN'S
AND FOLK SONGS

1. Allegro.

If there were cherries, cherries, morellos, morellos,
Every little Slovak girl would be proud, would be proud.
If roses and lilies would bloom, would bloom,
Then our queen would get a husband, a husband.

The Slovaks are a Slav people closely related to the Czechs. They live in the eastern half of Czechoslovakia, which formerly represented North Hungary.

2. Andante.

Kite settled on the branch,
I look at the [river] Vah:
Not rarely, O lad,
I gazed after you.

A characteristic of Slovak folk music, particularly in the less ancient melodies, is the grouping of phrases into three in duple (2/4) meter, as well as *tempo giusto* (strict rhythm).

3. Allegretto.

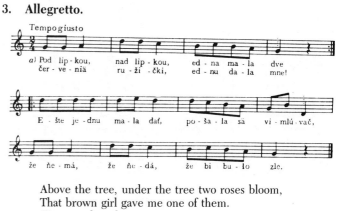

Above the tree, under the tree two roses bloom,
That brown girl gave me one of them.
Give me the other one,
Because it means love;
I won't give it, because there'll be none left for me.

4. Wedding Song. Andante.

Hey, Lado! Lado!*
For whom are you sewing
These clothes and slips, Mummy?
Hey, for you, for you,
My daughter,
For you are leaving me.

5. Variations. Molto andante.†

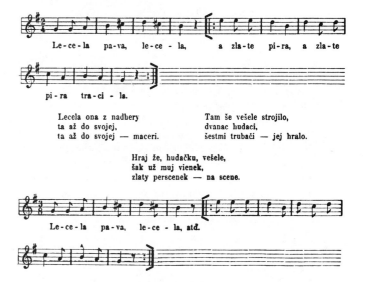

Lecela ona z nadbery
ta až do svojej
ta až do svojej — maceri.

Tam še vešele strojilo,
dvanac hudaci,
šestmi trubači — jej hralo.

Hraj že, hudačku, vešele,
šak už muj vienek,
zlaty perscenek — na scene.

*Lado is the Old Slavonic goddess of love.

†Note that Bartók, too, employs duple and triple-meter variants in his transcription of the folk tune.

*A magic formula (of pagan origin?) in this *regös* song (or carol) which is sung between Christmas and New Year.

Flew the peacock, flew,
His golden plume, his golden plume floated down.

He flew directly
To his, to his mother.

There was a merry company,
Twelve musicians, six trumpeters were playing.

Play merrily, musicians,
For my bridal wreath, my golden ring are on the wall.

6. Rondo. Allegro.

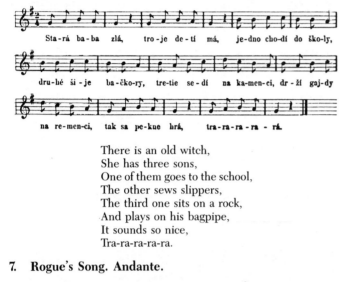

Stará baba zlá, troje detí má, jedno chodí do školy,
druhé šije bačkory, tretie sedí na kamenci, drží gajdy
na remenci, tak sa pekne hrá, tra-ra-ra-ra-rá.

> There is an old witch,
> She has three sons,
> One of them goes to the school,
> The other sews slippers,
> The third one sits on a rock,
> And plays on his bagpipe,
> It sounds so nice,
> Tra-ra-ra-ra-ra.

7. Rogue's Song. Andante.

Keď som išol z vojny z Dzindze-ša, z Dzindze-ša, ale ja s tym ži-dem
po-stre-tnul ja ži-da, co išol z va-ro-ša; ru-cel ja hun-cu-ta

ku vo-dze ku kra-ju
ži-da do Du-na-ju.

A išol tam, išol richtar z Bardiova,
vzal on teho žida huncuta na koňa.
Dunajova voda s Tisu še schodzela,
co ona huncuta žida vyrucela.

A jak on tam išol do solgabirova,
u teho tam bula šibeň už hotova.
U solgabirova tam ma vešac mali:
buli tam dzivčata a te ma nedaly.

When I came from the war, from Krakow, from Krakow,
I met a Jew who came from the city;
I went with him to the water, to the riverside,
I threw the wily Jew into the Danube.

Waters of the Danube flow into the Tisza,
They washed the wily Jew onto the riverside,
The village mayor of Bardiov happened to pass that way,
He put the wily Jew on the back of his horse.

Then he carried him, carried him to the sheriff,
There was the gallow tree prepared for my hanging.
The sheriff, the sheriff wanted to hang me,
But there were girls there who did not allow it.

8. Dance Song. Allegro.

Hej, na pre-šov-skej tur-ni dva ho-lub-ky še-dza, hej, ľu-dze
jim za-vi-dza, že še ra-dzi vi-dza.

Hej, ľudze, hej, preľudze,
nezavidzte teho,
hej, jaka to šumna vec,
chto rad vidzi keho.

Hey, two pigeons sit on the tower of Prešov,
Hey, people are watching them with envy, with envy.

Hey, people, hey, people, don't watch them that way,
Hey, there is no prettier thing than to love each other.

9. Children's Song. Andante.

Za-be-lej sa, za-be-lej, za-be-lej, v tej si-ho-ti
ze-le-nej, ze-le-nej.

> Unfold yourself, blossom, blossom,
> You green, verdant shrubs of the island.

10. Mourning Song. Largo.

Andantino.

V mi-ku-láš-skej kom-pa-ni-i le-ží mi-lý po-rú-ba-ný,
le-ží, le-ží za-bi-tý, roz-ma-rí-nom pri-kry-tý.

Zvoňte, zvony, na vše strany,
umrelo mi potešeni;
[:odpadnul mi z ruže kvet,
bude plakať celý svet.:]

In the barracks of Mikuláš
My dead lover is laid out;
He lies, he lies full of wounds,
Covered with rosemary.

Ring the bells in the whole country,
I am an orphan forever;
My rosebush is withered,
The whole world must mourn for him.

11. Lento.

> On the field of Bystrov
> Three roses are blooming, hoya hoy!
> They are so far from here,
> Yet I can smell their fragrance, O my God!

> Smell sweet, smell sweet for me,
> Sweet-smelling rose, hoya hoy!
> You gave your fragrance to me
> For three years, O my God!

The MS is from Bartók's Slovak folk-song collection, where it is classified as a "dotted" (that is, syncopated) rhythm melody. This type of melody, in which the syncopation occurs at the end of the melody sections or lines (bars 2, 4–5, 7, last measure), is characteristic of the more recent Hungarian folk songs and developed under Hungarian influence.

12. Poco andante.

Šuhajova mati,
ej, tak mi dobre nepraj,
kade ja chodievam,
tie chodníčky neklaj.

Mother of my lover,
Hey, she means me well;
Whichever way I go,
She curses my path.

Mother of my lover,
Hey, do not mean me well;
Whichever way I go,
Don't curse my path.

13. Allegro.

Zašly ti za vodienku, zmáčal som košelienku, zmáčal, zmáčal,
keď som si ja k mojej milej kráčal, kráčal.

Anička Mlynárova,
Where are your geese, where, where?
They have gone, gone across the river.

I went into the water,
My shirt got wet, got wet,
When I go to my sweetheart, it will be better, better.

14. Moderato.

Plowing, plowing are six oxen,
On the pine-topped hill.

Four are plowing, two harrowing,
Who is driving them?

15. Bagpipe Tune. Molto tranquillo.

Dance, maiden, dance,
Till your boots are tattered.
Your darling is a cobbler,
He will mend them for you,
Dance, dance, dance.

16. Lament. Lento.

The text translation is unsuitable for publication.

17. Andante.

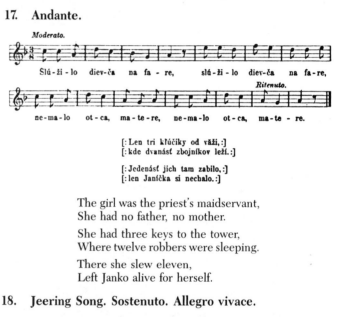

[: Len tri kľúčiky od váži,:]
[:kde dvanásť zbojníkov leží.:]

[:Jedenásť jich tam zabilo,:]
[:len Janíčka si nechalo.:]

The girl was the priest's maidservant,
She had no father, no mother.

She had three keys to the tower,
Where twelve robbers were sleeping.

There she slew eleven,
Left Janko alive for herself.

18. Jeering Song. Sostenuto. Allegro vivace.

Once I was your lover, gladly,
Now I am your comrade, but who cares?
If I go out to the street,
I will find an ape like you, better than you,
I don't need you!

19. Romance. Assai lento.

Dobrý večer vám, pani krčmárka;
či tu nebola moja frajerka?
frajerka?

Ej, bola, bola, za dverma stála;
šla by tancovať, ale sa bála,
ej, bála.

Bird on the branch, on the sorrowful branch,
I am so sad: my lover is far away, far away.

Good evening, landlady, good evening, landlady,
Was my darling here today, here today?

Hey, she was here, she was, she stood at the door,
She would have danced, had she not been afraid, hey, she was afraid.

20. Frisky. Prestissimo.

Don't go at dawn, Hanulienka, to the thorny bush, to the thorny bush,
Because your flounced skirt will get torn there, it will get torn there.

21. Funny Story. Allegro moderato.

2. Upékli jej pec chleba, šetko ona pojella.	6. Upékli jej dva voli, ňeňechala len rohi.	10. Doňésli jej vár piva, šetko ona vipila.
3. = 1.	7. = 1.	11. Salla dole, plakala, žebi ona zas pila.
4. Upékli jej druhú pec, ňeňechala len skrojec.	8. Upékli jej dve ovce, ňeňechala len zvonce.	12. Doňésli jej druhí vár, ňeňechala len pohár.
5. = 1.	9. Salla dole, plakala, že bi ona už pila.	13.—16. — — — — —

She flew down and was in tears, ay, yay, was in tears,
That she did not get fed, ay, yay, did not get fed.

She was given a whole bread, ay, yay, a whole bread,
She ate it one one piece, ay, yay, in one piece.

She flew down . . . [etc.]

She was given some more bread,
She emptied the whole oven.

She flew down . . . [etc.]

She was given two oxen,
She only left their horns behind.

She flew down . . . [etc.]

She was given two lambs,
She only left their bells behind.

She flew down and was in tears,
That she did not get anything to drink.

She was given a bucket of beer,
She emptied it all at once.

She flew down . . . [etc.]

She was given another bucket,
Only the bucket remained.*

22. Revelry. Molto allegro.

*The continuation is unsuitable for publication.

The lads caught a goat, they found him in the forest:
I will go there to ask them whether my darling is well.

23. Molto rubato, non troppo lento.

2. Aňi kukuk, aňi sova,
aňi sojka klebetná,
ňebuďe mä zo sna zbúďäč
lastoviška štebotná.

I am already an old shepherd,
I shall not live till spring,
The cuckoo will not call to me
From the top of the fence.

Neither the owl, nor the cuckoo,
Nor the magpie will call to me,
And the little twittering swallow
Nevermore will wake me.

24. Poco andante.

2. Stúpiv som tam na skalu,
na skalu stuďenú.

3. Pod tou skalou studňička
pila z ňej Zuzička.

I passed through the forest,
The forest of pine.

I stepped on a stone,
On a cold stone.

Under the stone is a well,
Zuzička drank from it.

25. Andante.

The text translation is unavailable.*

26. Scherzando. Allegretto.

*According to the remark in the Appendix to Vol. III (p. I) of *For Children*, the text of melody No. 19, "Datel' na dube" [Bird on the branch], is also sung to No. 25.

The text translation is unsuitable for publication.

27. Jeering Song. Allegro.

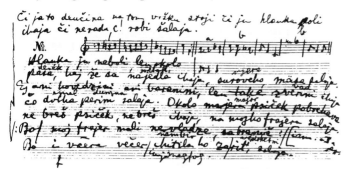

The text translation is unsuitable for publication.

28. Shepherd's Flute. Andante molto rubato.

The *fujera* (*fujara*; Hungarian: *hosszú furulya*) is a wooden peasant-flute, about 25–30 inches long, and is generally provided with five fingerholes.

29. Another Joke. Allegro.

The text is incomplete and its translation is unsuitable for publication.

30. Lament. Andante, molto rubato.

I have wandered a lot,
At night and on bumpy roads;
There was cold and mud,
But I never minded them,
I spent the nights with girls.

31. Canon. Poco vivace.

The text translation is unsuitable for publication.

32. Bagpipe Tune. Vivace.

Little garden, little garden,
Lettuce grows in it;
My darling, Janiček,
Let us love each other,
My mother doesn't care.

33. The Orphan. Poco andante.*

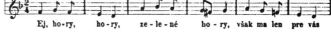

Ej, bolí, bolí, aj pobolíva,
srdenko plače, až tak omdlíva.

Ej, hory, hory, zelené hory,
kde sa podeli rodiče moji?

Rodiče moji dávno umreli,
a mňa, sirotku, tu zanechali.

Hey, forest, forest, green forest,
Your pain fills my head.

Hey, pain fills my head,
My heart cries, they have left me.

Hey, forest, forest, green forest,
Where have my parents gone?

My parents have died long ago,
They left me, an orphan, alone.

34. Romance. Poco allegretto.

2. [: V tom hájičku domíček,
malí ňeveliki :], -velikí

*Nos. 33 and 34 were arranged by Emma Gruber (née Sándor: d. 1958), a pianist, composer and folk-song collector who studied counterpoint with Bartók a number of years prior to his appointment as Professor of Piano at the Academy of Music in Budapest in 1907. In 1910 she married Bartók's best friend, the famed Hungarian composer Zoltán Kodály, and for many years her home was the meeting place for those musicians who were devoted to the exploration of new trends in composition.

I know a little forest,
It is small, not big.

In the little forest is a little house,
It is small, not big, not big.

35. Highwayman's Tune. Allegro.

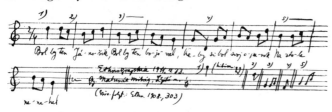

Jánošik* is a big bully,
He would beat me sorely,
If only he had not forgotten
His belt (at home) on the table.

36. Largo.

If I knew where my darling
Mows hay in the morning,
I would bring him roses
In my apron.

37. Molto tranquillo.†

The Danube's bank is green at Bratislava,
They are exercising the lads there.

I was exercised by my darling,
I had to go to her for three years.

In the fourth year the captain came,
He saddled a horse under me.

My horse, my horse, you are saddled already?
O my God! I am sitting on you!

*A notorious robber chieftain.

†This song, a popular one among the Slovak peasants, was probably derived from a Hungarian art song which also became popular among Hungarian, Slovak and Moravian peasants. Note, in bars 5 and 7, the so-called Slovakian rhythm-contraction: the text syllables of bars 2–3, 9–10 are compressed rhythmically into one-bar lengths.

38. Farewell. Adagio.

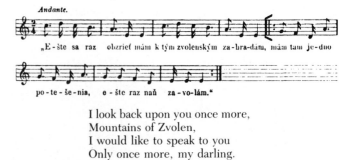

I look back upon you once more,
Mountains of Zvolen,
I would like to speak to you
Only once more, my darling.

39. Ballad. Poco largo.

2. Prišli k ňemu hájňici,
   dolnozemskí zbojňíci:

3. —Daj dó šuhaj, halinu,
   dau si nám pásť järinu.

4. —Jä si halinu ňedám,
   jä sa s vami pojednám.

5. Ak sa oni jednali,
   präm Janíčka zabili.

6. Leží Janík zabití,
   rozmajrínom prikrití.

Janko drives out two oxen,
Hey! Janko drives out two oxen,
He drives them out to the pasture.

The highwaymen went up to him,
Hey! The highwaymen went up to him,
The highwaymen of the plains.

Give us your *halina* [cape], lad,
Hey! Give us your *halina*, lad,
Give us your aftergrass, too.

I won't give you my *halina*,
Hey! I won't give you my *halina*,
I'll make a bargain with you.

But they were not bargaining,
Hey! But they were not bargaining,
They killed Janko there.

Janko is lying, he is dead,
Hey! Janko is lying, he is dead,
He is covered with rosemary.

40 & 41. Rhapsody. Parlando, molto rubato. Allegro moderato.*

Hey! Blow, you summer wind,
Bring with you the sweet smell.

*No. 40 is a shepherd's song (*valaská*, also known as *detvanská* [from the village of Detva, in the Zvolen district of Slovakia]), probably dating back to ancient times. The autochthonous Slovak structure consists of an improvisation-like melody made up of six-syllable text lines, in *parlando- rubato* (that is, free) rhythm.

Clouds in the sky,
Wet the ground with dew.

Hey! Green forest
With tinseled trees,
If you saw my darling,
You would bring her to me.

The source melody to No. 41 is unavailable. Its text:

Hey, what a beautiful
House is this county hall.
Hey, will you sit there,
Janko, some day?

Janiček Vršovský,
Don't go without your axe!
Hey, you are worth as much as
Seven other lads.

I have no fear alone,
If seven would come!
Hey, even twelve can come,
I will thrash my way out of it.

42. Mourning Song. Lento.

The text is not in conformity with the character of the melody, and its translation is unavailable.

43. Funeral Song. Lento.

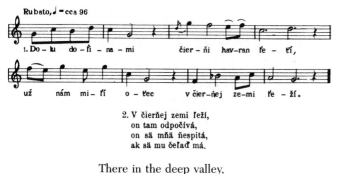

2. V čierňej zemi leží,
on tam odpočíva,
on sä mňä ňespitá,
ak sä mu čeľad má.

There in the deep valley,
Hey, there the black raven flies;
There my dear father lies,
Hey, under the black earth.

Under the black earth,
Hey, he reposes quietly;
He will never ask me,
Hey, how are you, my servant?

REMARKS: Bartók's use of the designation *attacca* indicates that pieces so marked are to be played as a group. The following melodies, therefore, should be performed as a suite of pieces:

Vols. I & II (Hungarian tunes): XIII–XIV–XV; XVIII–XIX; XX–XXI; XXXIII–XXXIV; and XXXVI–XXXVII–XXXVIII.

Vols. III & IV (Slovak tunes): 1–2–3; 11–12–13; 16–17; and 23–24–25.

His recordings (listed below) show the following groupings from the first two volumes: III, IV, VI, X, XII; XIII, XV, XVIII, XIX, XXI; and XXVI, XXXVI, XXXIII, XXXII.

REFERENCES
(see list at end of Introduction for full titles)
Ujfalussy, *Béla Bartók*, pp. 85–98.
Suchoff (ed.), *Béla Bartók Essays*, No. 59 (pp. 426–430). See also the various essays on Hungarian and Slovak folk songs and instrumental music.
Suchoff, *Guide to the Mikrokosmos*, pp. 11–15.
Viski, *Hungarian Dances*, pp. 63–73.
Stevens, *Life and Music*, pp. 114–115.
Memorial Review, pp. 62–64.
Complete Edition, LPX 11394–95.
For Children: Picture Book, Colorvox 33.
Béla Bartók [the composer at the piano], Vox 650–651, Cl.C 2075-2076 (incomplete), Polydor Vox PLP 6010, Turnabout Vox TV 4159.

THREE BURLESQUES, OP. 8C

COMPOSITION DATES: No. 1: 27 November 1908. No. 2: May 1911. No. 3: 1910.

FIRST PERFORMANCE: Budapest, 12 November 1921 (the complete work).*

FIRST PUBLICATION: Rózsavölgyi és Társa, Budapest, 1912.

During the late spring of 1944 Bartók revised the *Three Burlesques* when his publisher, Boosey & Hawkes, decided to reprint the Hungarian edition.

Burlesque No. 1, "Quarrel," is dedicated to Márta Ziegler, Bartók's first wife, whom he married in the autumn of 1909. Márta was a former piano pupil of the composer (at that time Bartók was Professor of Piano at the Budapest Conservatory of Music), and a draft of the piece—apparently written for her by Bartók—shows this amusing entry: "Please choose one of the titles: 'Anger because of an interrupted visit' or '*Rondoletto à capriccio*' or 'Vengeance is sweet' or 'Play it if you can' or 'November 27.'"

The first, sketch draft—also untitled and with *Prestissimo* as the tempo designation (see p. 81 in this volume)—shows the following performance comments: bar 1—"angrily"; bar 60—"with a weeping voice (considerable slackening)"; bar 73—"gradually increasing speed"; bar 88—"sorrowfully"; bar 99—"diminishing voice."

Burlesque No. 2, "Slightly Tipsy," was a perennial favorite of the composer for concert programs. He recorded it for the His Majesty's Voice label (G.AM 2622), and he transcribed it for orchestra as the fourth movement of *Hungarian Sketches* (1931). In his 1944 revision Bartók deleted from bar 14 the performance comment which appears (in Hungarian) in the original edition: "with indifference."

Perhaps Bartók's predilection for this piece stems from its thematic link to musical folklore. The melody (upward-beamed notes in bars 1-4) represents a specific level in Bartók's compositional procedure for the transmutation of folk music into art music: creating a theme in imitation of a genuine folk tune. The following Hungarian folk song, a dance tune designated by the peasant performer as "Bagpipes Polka," has structural features identical with Bartók's invention: four seven-syllable melody sections, the first three melody sections ending on the third degree of the Mixolydian mode; ABAB content-structure; isometric rhythm schema in duple meter; and approximately the same metronome mark.

*Bartók played one of the pieces in Tîrgu Mureş, Rumania, on 20 April 1912; two of them in Kecskemét, Hungary, on 1 February 1913; and Burlesque No. 3 (in Budapest?) on 27 March 1921.

Your grandmother is very kind,
In winter a foal, in summer a horse,
And when she sits by the hearth
They all call: "Whoa! my horse, whoa!"

Burlesque No. 3 [*Capriccioso*] has no extramusical subtitle to indicate its program. But there are figurations and other musical attributes that seem to echo those in Bagatelle No. 14, subtitled "My Dancing Sweetheart," which Bartók wrote in the early part of 1908 as a kind of musical memento of a traumatic event in his life: the bitter ending of his relationship with the eminent young Hungarian violinist Stefi Geyer. In fact it was perhaps in 1911, the year after he composed the third Burlesque, that Bartók orchestrated Bagatelle No. 14 as the second, "Grotesque" movement of *Two Portraits*, op. 5.*

REFERENCES:

Demény (ed.), *Béla Bartók Letters*, p. 339.
Kroó, *Guide to Bartók*, pp. 51–55.
Stevens, *Life and Music*, pp. 116–117.
Complete Edition, LPX 11336, 11355.
Béla Bartók at the Piano [Burlesque No. 2], Bartók Recording Studio BRS 003 (also recorded on BRS 903, HMV G.AN 2622).

FOUR DIRGES, OP. 9A

COMPOSITION DATES: Nos. 1, 3, 4: 1910. No. 2: 1909.

FIRST PERFORMANCE: Budapest, 17 October 1917 (Nos. 1 and 2; by Ernő Dohnányi).

FIRST PUBLICATION: Rózsavölgyi és Társa, Budapest, 1912.

Dirge No. 2, the first piece composed in the work, was later transcribed for orchestra and retitled "Melodie" (No. 3 in *Hungarian Sketches for Orchestra*, 1931). The set of *Four Dirges* was originally and erroneously published as Opus 8c, instead of 9a in accordance with the composer's intention.

The music represents a further outcome of Bartók's intensive study, begun in the fall of 1907, of the innovative creations of Claude Debussy. The first evidence of this study can be seen in Bartók's piano composition, Bagatelle No. 4, composed in 1908, which is simply a transcription of an Old Hungarian pentatonic folk song harmonized in French Impressionist style.

This folk song is also the melodic source for Dirge No. 2:

Apparently the Dirge theme was molded from the folk tune by a process of addition and subtraction of notes (Mm. 1–7 contain thirteen notes, the folk song has eight), thereby creating an imitation form. The essential pentatonic flavor is retained but, on the other hand, the use of ¾ time and 13-syllable melodic structure are unknown in the old-style Hungarian folk music to which the source melody belongs.

*In a letter to the pianist Ernő Balogh, dated 4 October 1944, in connection with the proposed recordings of various works, Bartók estimates the performance time for each of the Burlesques as two minutes.

Coincidentally—perhaps otherwise?—the folk-song text is a "lament" by a cowherd whose cattle wandered off while he slept in the barn!

Another coincidence can be found in Dirge No. 4, whose opening bars are similar to—indeed, with the identical chords!—those in Debussy's tenth Prelude (Book I) for piano.

Bartók: Dirge No. 4

Debussy: Prelude No. 10

Both pieces were composed in 1910 or, at least, completed during that year. In fact Bartók's Dirge may have antedated Debussy's Prelude. The parallel development of the two men is evident in these two piano miniatures. Later on, in the 1920s, the Debussy harmonic concepts were integrated in Bartók's work with structural features derived from Beethoven and contrapuntal techniques stemming from Bach and his Italian predecessors and contemporaries (for example, Frescobaldi and Della Ciaia), all fused with elements from East European musical folklore in what was to become the characteristic but uniquely Bartókian style of composition.

REFERENCES:

Ujfalussy, *Béla Bartók*, pp. 71–75, 79–84, 93–94.
Suchoff (ed.), *Béla Bartók Essays*, pp. 317, 335, 362, 479–480, 505, 518.
Demény (ed.), *Béla Bartók Letters*, pp. 207, 411.
Suchoff, *Guide to the Mikrokosmos*, p. 95.
Stevens, *Life and Music*, pp. 40–41, 45–46, 113–114, 119–120.
Memorial Review, p. 62.
Complete Edition, LPX 11335.

TWO PICTURES, OP. 10

COMPOSITION DATE: August 1910.

FIRST PERFORMANCE: Budapest, 25 February 1913 (orchestral version).

FIRST PUBLICATION: Rózsavölgyi és Társa, Budapest, 1912.

When Bartók drafted the orchestral version of *Two Pictures* he titled the work in Hungarian (*Két kép*) and French (*Deux images*). His use of *Images*—like Debussy's with his set of three piano pieces in 1905—could be considered as a kind of homage, in acknowledgment of his musical debt to the French composer. In view of the thematic content and, moreover, the forward-looking second movement, *Two Pictures* might better be considered as a kind of farewell to Debussy's style as a primary shaping force in Bartók's oeuvre.

1. In Full Flower.

This movement is remarkably similar to Debussy's "Nuages" (Clouds), the first of three *Nocturnes for Orchestra*. The main difference, other than the use of more dissonant sonorities, is in thematic construction. As in Dirge No. 2, there is a transformed Hungarian folk-style melody as the B theme (the movement is in ABA form), beginning on the fifth beat of bar 37 and ending on the sixth beat of bar 40 (repeated in bars 41–43).

Analysis of this theme discloses an essentially pentatonic structure, "dotted" (that is, syncopated) rhythm pattern, and—as the phrase marks indicate—the equivalent of four seven-syllable melody sections. These features are characteristic of Old Hungarian folk-song style.

The first theme, on the other hand (bars 1–9), seems to stem from Slovak folk-song material: four five-syllable melody sections and, especially, the Lydian mode (a major scale with the augmented fourth degree). Beginning in 1906 Bartók collected many specimens of this structure among the Slovak minorities living in what was then Greater Hungary.

At the Coda (bar 75) Bartók stresses the whole-tone scale, thus following Debussy's innovative harmonic path of interrelating the Lydian mode with the pentatonic and whole-tone scales.

2. Village Dance.

This movement, in rondo form (ABACA), has thematic material that is remarkably similar to Rumanian instrumental folk-music style. In point of fact the tonal and rhythmic structure is that of the Bihor County (Transylvania) music "dialect" that Bartók discovered during his 1909–1910 travels to collect Rumanian folk-music materials. This "dialect" has, as main features, the Lydian mode with a minor seventh degree (for example, a scale beginning on F, with B-natural and E-flat) and the rhythm schema of three notes—an eighth plus two sixteenths.

This dance movement differs from Bartók's *Two Rumanian Dances for Piano*, composed between 1909 and 1910, in that the thematic transformations approximate a peculiar melodic style Bartók found in Transylvanian villages. This style consists of a string of related two- or four-bar motifs that are usually repeated without any plan or order, and whose range generally spans a pentachord.

The relationship to the first movement can be seen in harmonic terms. The whole-tone scale appears in bars 19–20 and 23–24, and the pentatonic configuration occurs in bars 68–69 and 72–73 and in the second line on p. 128.

In summary, the *Two Pictures*, though sharply contrasted in seemingly opposite ways, are integrated through the medium of tonal language. And the "Village Dance" points the way of the future Bartók, in which the atmosphere of rural folk music is to be the pervading influence rather than artificial harmonic or other musical constructions.

REFERENCES

Ujfalussy, *Béla Bartók*, pp. 95–97, 121.
Suchoff (ed.), *Béla Bartók Essays*, pp. 106–108, 116, 244–268.
Demény (ed.), *Béla Bartók Letters*, p. 410.
Kroó, *Guide to Bartók*, pp. 56–59.
Suchoff, *Guide to the Mikrokosmos*, pp. 36, 47–48, 101, 117–118.
Stevens, *Life and Music*, pp. 41, 266–267.
Memorial Review, p. 62.
Complete Edition, LPX 1302.

THE FIRST TERM AT THE PIANO

COMPOSITION DATE: 1913 (probably during the early part of the year).

FIRST PUBLICATION: Rózsavölgyi és Társa, Budapest, 1913.

In 1912 the publisher asked Bartók, then Professor of Piano at the Budapest Academy of Music, to construct a piano method that would serve as instructional material from the beginning to the highest degree of study. Since Bartók was inexperienced in the various aspects of elementary piano pedagogy, he asked Sándor Reschofsky (a colleague on the Academy's piano faculty) to collaborate in the undertaking.

According to Reschofsky's memoirs, the two authors agreed not to specify which parts of the resultant *Piano School (Zongora Iskola)* each would contribute. In the spring of 1913 the first volume of the planned series was ready for the press. The basic framework and finger exercises were written by Reschofsky; Bartók composed the related pieces which are designated by metronome marks (exception: No. 92, for which the metronome mark was inadvertently omitted).*

Apparently five volumes were produced: Nos. 2 and 5 by Reschofsky, No. 4 by Dr. Sándor Kovács, and No. 3—*Thirteen Little Piano Pieces (from Anna Magdalena Bach's Notebook)* by J. S. Bach—edited by Bartók as his only other contribution to the project. In 1929 he selected eighteen of the pieces he had composed for *Piano School* and had them published under the present title.

1. **Moderato.**
2. **Moderato.**

These two pieces are, respectively, Nos. 21 and 22 in the *Piano School (Zongora Iskola)*.

3. **Dialogue. Moderato.**
4. **Dialogue. Moderato.**

Nos. 24 and 26 in the *Piano School* and untitled there.

5. **Moderato.**
6. **Moderato.**

Nos. 36 and 40 in the *Piano School*.

7. **Folk Song. Moderato.**

No. 44 in the *Piano School*. The source melody has not been identified.

8. **Andante.**
9. **Andante.**

Nos. 51 and 59 in the *Piano School*.

10. **Hungarian Folk Song. Allegro.**

Erzsi Virág her bed
Has made very high,
Gábor Váczi his hat
Has forgotten on it.

This is a teasing song to pair off a courting couple. It corresponds to No. 68 in the *Piano School* and No. 74 (Vol. III) in Bartók's *Mikrokosmos* for Piano Solo (1926–1939). The *Mikrokosmos* transcription is completely different from the earlier (1913) version of the tune.

11. **Minuet. Andante.**

No. 89 in the *Piano School*.

12. **Swineherd's Dance. Allegro.**

No. 77 in the *Piano School*. The folk-tune source has not been

*The work was reprinted in 1968 (Boosey & Hawkes, London) with English translation of the Hungarian text by Leslie Russell.

identified. See the commentary on *For Children*, Part One, XXXIX, above, for a description of this kind of dance melody.

13. Hungarian Folk Song. Andante.

No. 95 in the *Piano School*. The song, which was collected in 1912 in the Transylvanian village of Gyanta (Bihor County), belongs to the mixed style (Class C; see the opening commentary to *For Children* above) of Hungarian folk-music material.

14. Andante.

No. 105 in the *Piano School*, where it appears in the key of G.

15. Wedding Song. Moderato.

The cart rattles, Jancsi cracks his whip!
Perhaps they come for me!
Alas, dear mother, beloved one who nursed me,
Soon they'll carry me away.

No. 116 in the *Piano School*. This piece, too, is a mixed-style (Class C) Hungarian folk song, sung when the cart arrives at the house of the bride's parents to carry her and her dowry to the bridegroom's house. Because of the pentatonic structure of the tune, the song could also be considered as an old-style (Class A) folk tune.

16. Peasant's Dance. Allegro moderato.

No. 115 in the *Piano School*. An old-style Hungarian folk tune, with mixed-style structural features (Bartók originally placed the tune in Class C of his Hungarian folk-song collection). In the Mixolydian mode, that is, a major scale with a minor seventh (the accompaniment, however, is in G major!).

The source melody, unavailable for reproduction here, was recorded by Béla Vikár, the first Hungarian ethnomusicologist to use recording equipment, and transcribed by Bartók.

17. Allegro deciso.
18. Waltz. Tempo di Valse.

Nos. 118 and 119 in the *Piano School*.

REFERENCES
Suchoff, *Guide to the Mikrokosmos*, pp. 8, 38, 52–54, 65–66.
Complete Edition, SLPX 11336.

SONATINA

COMPOSITION DATE: 1915.

FIRST PERFORMANCE: Perhaps Berlin, Germany, 8 March 1920.

FIRST PUBLICATION: Rózsavölgyi és Társa, Budapest, 1919.

The *Sonatina* is based on five Rumanian folk tunes that Bartók collected from peasants and Gypsies in Transylvanian villages, from February 1910 to April 1914. He later transcribed the composition for orchestra (*Transylvanian Dances*, 1931).

On 2 July 1944, during the "Ask the Composer" concert-program broadcast (Station WNYC) from the Brooklyn Museum, Bartók made the following comments prior to the performance of the work by his wife, Edith Pásztory-Bartók:

> This sonatina was originally conceived as a group of Rumanian folk dances for piano. The three parts which Mrs. Bartók will play were selected from a group and given the present title of *Sonatina*. The first movement, which is called "Bagpipers," is a

dance—these are two dances played by two bagpipe players, the first by one and the second by another. The second movement is called "Bear Dance"—this was played for me by a peasant violinist on the G and D strings, on the lower strings in order to have it more similar to a bear's voice. Generally the violin players use the E string. And the last movement contains also two folk melodies played by peasant violin players.

1. Bagpipers.

The first movement is in ABA form. The A theme is melody No. 42 from Bartók's study *Rumanian Folk Music*, Vol. I; the B theme (*Allegro*) is No. 639 from the same book. The designation *ardeleana* (= Transylvanian) indicates that the tune is to be performed for a round dance, in two parts, and danced by two women and a man.

©1967 by Martinus Nijhoff, The Hague.

2. Bear Dance.

A boys' dance from Maramureş County (the northern part of Transylvania). The source melody, played on the violin by an old Gypsy man and accompanied by a two-string guitar strummed in a rhythm of equal eighths, is published in *Rumanian Folk Music*, Vol. IV, melody No. 171:

©1975 by Martinus Nijhoff, The Hague.

3. Finale.

The last movement is in AB form, with a short reprise of both themes at the coda (*tranquillo*). Theme A, designated *A Turcii* in *Rumanian Folk Music* (Vol. I, No. 107), indicates a solo dance by a man, called the *turca*, who wears a peculiar type of animal head with a movable beak. As he dances he operates the beak by means of a string so that a clattering sound is produced in time with the rhythm of the music.

The *A Turcii* is performed during the winter solstice (Christmas time). The tune apparently may be used for the *mărunţel*, a dance for couples.

The B theme (*Sostenuto*) appears as melody No. 7 in *Rumanian Folk Music*, Vol. I, where it is designated *Babaleuca* (a description of this dance is missing). Both source melodies are unaccompanied violin pieces:

©1967 by Martinus Nijhoff, The Hague.

REFERENCES

Suchoff (ed.), *Béla Bartók Essays*, pp. 103, 112, 115–118, 122, 253, 262.
Demény (ed.), *Béla Bartók Letters*, pp. 203, 220, 339, 396.
Kroó, *Guide to Bartók*, pp. 70–73.
Suchoff, *Guide to the Mikrokosmos*, pp. 47–48, 119–120.
Stevens, *Life and Music*, pp. 123–124.
Bartók, *Rumanian Folk Music*, Vol. I, pp. 15–17, 19–23, 35, 40–41, 46–50; Vol. IV, pp. 29–30, 34–36.
Complete Edition, SLPX 11336.

REFERENCES

Bibliography

Bartók, Béla. *The Hungarian Folk Song*. Edited by Benjamin Suchoff. Albany: State University of New York Press, 1981.
——.*Rumanian Folk Music*. Edited by Benjamin Suchoff. The Hague: Martinus Nijhoff, 1967 (Vols. I–III), 1975 (Vols. IV–V).
——.*Slovenské L'udové Piesne*. Edited by Alica and Oskár Elschek. Bratislava: Slovenská Akadémia Vied, 1959 (Vol. I), 1970 (Vol. II).
Demény, János (ed.). *Béla Bartók Letters*. London: Faber & Faber, 1971.
Kroó, György. *A Guide to Bartók*. Budapest: Corvina Press, 1974.
A Memorial Review. New York: Boosey & Hawkes, Inc., 1950.
Stevens, Halsey. *The Life and Music of Béla Bartók*. New York: Oxford University Press, 1964.
Suchoff, Benjamin (ed.) *Béla Bartók Essays*. London and New York: Faber & Faber and St. Martin's Press, 1976.
——.*Guide to the Mikrokosmos of Béla Bartók*. London: Boosey & Hawkes, 1971.
Ujfalussy, József. *Béla Bartók*. Budapest: Corvina Press, 1971.
Viski, Károly. *Hungarian Dances*. London: Simpkin Marshall, 1937.

Discography

Béla Bartók [the composer at the piano]. New York: Vox 650–651, Polydor Vox PLP 6010, Turnabout Vox TV 4159. Paris: Cl.C 2075–2076.
Béla Bartók at the Piano. London: HMV G.AN 2622. New York: Bartók Recording Studio 003, 903.
Complete Edition Bartók Béla. Budapest: Hungaroton LPX 1302, 11335, 11336, 11355, 11394–95 (two records).
For Children: Picture Book. Budapest: Colorvox 33 (two records).

First MS page of "Chain, chain," No. XII, Part One, of *For Children* (page 11).

MS of "If there were cherries," No. 1, Part Two, of *For Children* (page 41).

First MS page of "Quarrel," No. 1 of *Three Burlesques*, op. 8c (page 81).

MS of No. 1 of *Four Dirges*, op. 9a (page 100).

First MS page of "In Full Flower," No. 1 of *Two Pictures*, op. 10 (page 108).

Page of autograph sketches for sections of "Bagpipers" (No. 1) and "Finale" (No. 3) of *Sonatina* (pages 144 ff.).